CW01238985

HOW PEOPLE LIVE

ON THE MOVE

TESSA POTTER

Editorial planning
Jollands Editions

MACMILLAN EDUCATION

© Macmillan Education Limited 1987
© BLA Publishing Limited 1987

All rights reserved. No reproduction, copy or transmission of this publication may be made without written permission.

No paragraph of this publication may be reproduced, copied or transmitted save with written permission or in accordance with the provisions of the Copyright Act 1956 (as amended), or under the terms of any licence permitting limited copying issued by the Copyright Licensing Agency, 33 – 4 Alfred Place, London WC1E 7DP.

Any person who does any unauthorised act in relation to this publication may be liable to criminal prosecution and civil claims for damages.

First published 1987
Reprinted 1987

Published by
MACMILLAN EDUCATION LTD
Houndmills, Basingstoke, Hampshire RG21 2XS
and London
Companies and representatives
throughout the world

Designed and produced by BLA Publishing Limited,
Swan Court, East Grinstead, Sussex, England.

Also in LONDON · HONG KONG · TAIPEI · SINGAPORE · NEW YORK

A Ling Kee Company

Illustrations by Fiona Fordyce
   and BLA Publishing Limited
Colour origination by Waterden Reproductions Limited
Printed in Hong Kong

British Library Cataloguing in Publication Data

Potter, Tessa
   On the move. — (How people live)
   — (Macmillan world library)
   1. Nomads — Juvenile literature
   I. Title   II. Series
   307.7′72   GN387

ISBN 0-333-42622-3
ISBN 0-333-42620-7 Series

Acknowledgements
The Publishers wish to thank the following organizations for their invaluable assistance in the preparation of this book.

Canadian High Commission
Civil Aviation Authority
MGM/UA
National Film Archive
Overseas Containers Limited
Oxfam
P & O Cruises Limited

Photographic credits
t = top b = bottom l = left r = right

cover: ZEFA; The Hutchison Library

4 Bryan and Cherry Alexander; 5t, 5b, 6t, ZEFA; 6b Chris Fairclough; 7 Mansell Collection; 8/9 South American Pictures; 9, 10 Bryan and Cherry Alexander; 11t The Hutchison Library; 11b Canadian High Commission; 12/13 John Lythgoe/Seaphot; 13 ZEFA; 14t, 14b Bryan and Cherry Alexander; 15 Novosti Press Agency; 17t, 17b Bryan and Cherry Alexander; 18t Chris Fairclough; 18b ZEFA; 19 South American Pictures; 20t 20b, 21, 22t, 22b, 23 The Hutchison Library; 24, 25t, 25b Peter Johnson/NHPA; 26t The Hutchison Library; 26b, 27 Jeremy Hartley/Oxfam; 28, 29 Susan Griggs Agency; 30 Peter Johnson/NHPA; 31t ZEFA; 31b, 32t, 32b The Hutchison Library; 33 South American Pictures; 34 The Hutchison Library; 35t John Lythgoe/Seaphot; 35b South American Pictures; 36t ZEFA; 36b, 37t, 37b Chris Fairclough; 38 ZEFA; 39 David Redfern; 40 Dominic Photography; 40/41 MGM/UA; 42t, 42b Overseas Containers Limited; 43 P & O Cruises Limited; 44 Camerapix; 45t NASA; 45b Civil Aviation Authority

Note to the reader
In this book there are some words in the text which are printed in **bold** type. This shows that the word is listed in the glossary on page 46. The glossary gives a brief explanation of words which may be new to you.

Contents

Introduction	4	Moving with the seasons	28
Wanderers of the past	6	A village on the move	30
Where do nomads live?	8	Living in the forests	32
Homes and belongings	10	Working away from home	34
Nomads of the cold desert	12	Circus people	36
Following reindeer	14	Music on the move	38
Life in the Arctic	16	Nomads of the stage	40
Nomads of the hot desert	18	Nomads of the sea	42
The Bedouin today	20	Nomads of air and space	44
The Tuareg	22		
Living in the Kalahari	24	Glossary	46
At the edge of the desert	26	Index	48

Introduction

The first people who lived on Earth were **nomads**. They wandered from place to place looking for food and water. They lived by hunting animals and gathering food. They had to do this to **survive**. Later, some nomads kept cattle and sheep. They moved around with their animals looking for fresh **pasture** and water. These people were nomadic **herders**. In time, some people began to farm the land and grow their own food. Then they were able to **settle** in one place.

▼ **In northern Norway, there are still a few nomads. They are called Lapps, or Saami. They use snow scooters to tow their sledges.**

Nomads today

There are still a few nomads left in the world. These people are sometimes called true nomads. They do not want to settle. They prefer to keep on the move. They have to find food and water for themselves and their animals. They live in the world's most deserted places. These are places where no one else wants to live. The lives of these nomads have stayed the same for thousands of years. Oil and **minerals** have been found in many of these deserted places. This has changed the way of life of many of these people.

There are also people who lead a nomadic life for other reasons. Some people have to leave their homes and travel long distances to find work. Other people, such as circus workers and air crew, have to be on the move because of the work they do.

Introduction

▶ In some parts of the world there are few buses or trucks. As many people as possible get on them to travel from place to place.

▼ Many people travel by plane today. They may be travelling on business or going on holiday.

Travelling to find work

Some people cannot find work near their homes. They have to travel to countries who need workers. These people are called **migrant workers**. They stay away from home for several years. In some countries, they cannot go back to visit their families because they do not earn enough money. After a while, they return home to settle with their families.

Emigrants are people who leave their own countries to live and work in new countries. Many people have **emigrated** from Europe to the United States and Australia in the last 100 years. They hoped to find work and a better life.

5

Wanderers of the past

Our **ancestors** were always on the move. They roamed over the Earth to look for food and water. They hunted animals for food and skins. They gathered fruit, nuts and roots to eat. They moved around in small groups.

Some of these people crossed over the Bering Strait from Asia to North America. They may have followed wild animals over the frozen sea. Some of them settled in the forests of Canada. Others wandered south to live on the plains of North America. In time, some people reached South America. This was about 15 000 years ago.

Groups of nomads are also thought to have reached Australia from Asia. They were the first people to live there. The people from Europe who came to Australia later gave them a Latin name. They called them Aborigines (*Ab-or-ij-in-eez*) or 'the ones who were there from the beginning'.

▲ This Inuit (Eskimo) woman has dug a hole in the Arctic ice. She is catching fish with a line and bait. The Inuits have fished this way for hundreds of years.

▼ A few Aborigines in Australia still lead a nomadic life. They live on food they find in the bush. There are roots which they can cook and eat. Some plants can be used for making medicines.

Wanderers of the past

Settling down

About 5000 years ago, the nomads began to change their way of life. They started to sow seeds and grow their own food. They began to tame some animals instead of just following them. They kept their own herds near their homes. Now they had enough to eat without wandering far and wide.

This new way of life brought many changes for the people who settled down. They began to live in villages. The villages became towns. Some people started to make things. Then they began to exchange their goods for goods that they needed. They did not use money. This is how trade began.

The explorers

The first explorers were sailors and traders. They sailed out across the seas to find new lands and to buy and sell their goods. They found spices and gold.

Five hundred years ago, Christopher Columbus sailed from Spain across the Atlantic Ocean to find a way to India. When he reached America he thought the land was India. He called the people who lived there 'Indians'. More people from Europe went to other parts of North and South America. Some of them stayed there. Others took gold and treasure back to their own countries.

Over 200 years ago, Captain Cook landed on the east coast of Australia. He called the land he had found New South Wales.

More people from Europe went to live in America and then Australia. They started to farm the land. Without their hunting grounds, the Indians and Aborigines could not carry on their old way of life. Later, some of them were given land to live on, but by then their true way of live had been destroyed.

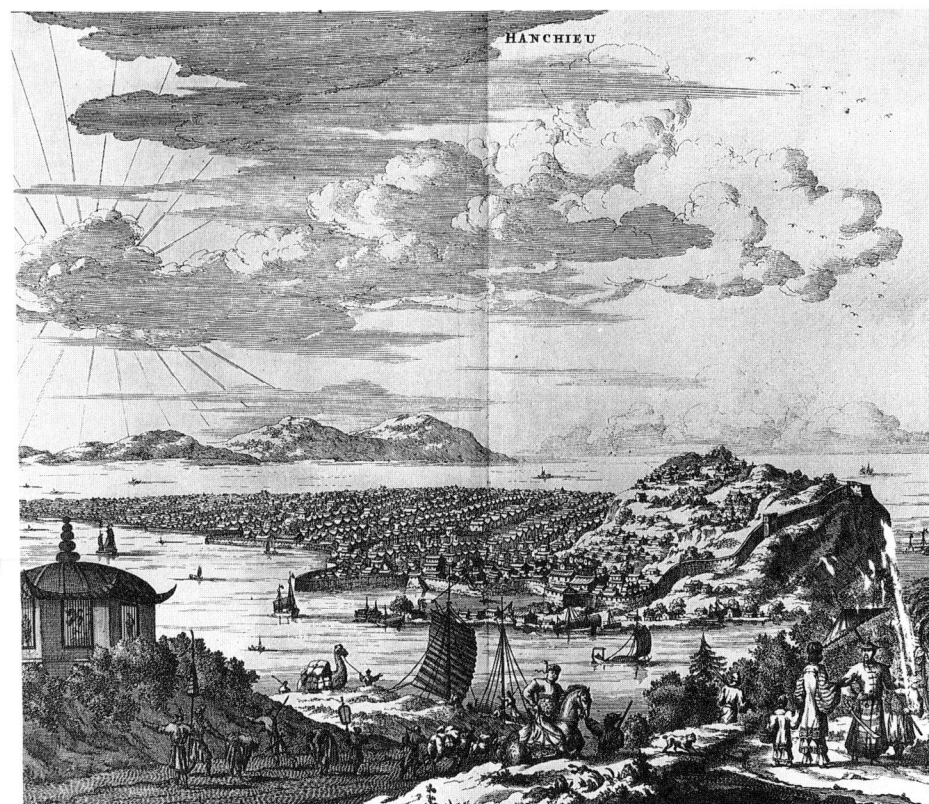

▶ People have traded goods around the world for hundreds of years. This is the harbour of Hankow in China, 300 years ago. Goods are being unloaded from a Dutch ship.

Where do nomads live?

The weather, or **climate**, changes from one part of the world to another. Most people in the world live in places where it is neither too hot nor too cold. The climate in these parts of the world is called **temperate**. In these temperate parts of the world there is always enough rain to grow **crops**. There is good grassland for animals to feed on.

There are some parts of the world where very few people live. The climate is either too hot or too cold. There is not enough rain for crops to grow. There is not enough grass to feed cattle. These places are the **desert** lands of the world.

A few nomads still live in these hot and cold deserts. Some of them still follow a way of life that is thousands of years old. It is a hard life, and they can only survive by moving around. They cannot settle in one place.

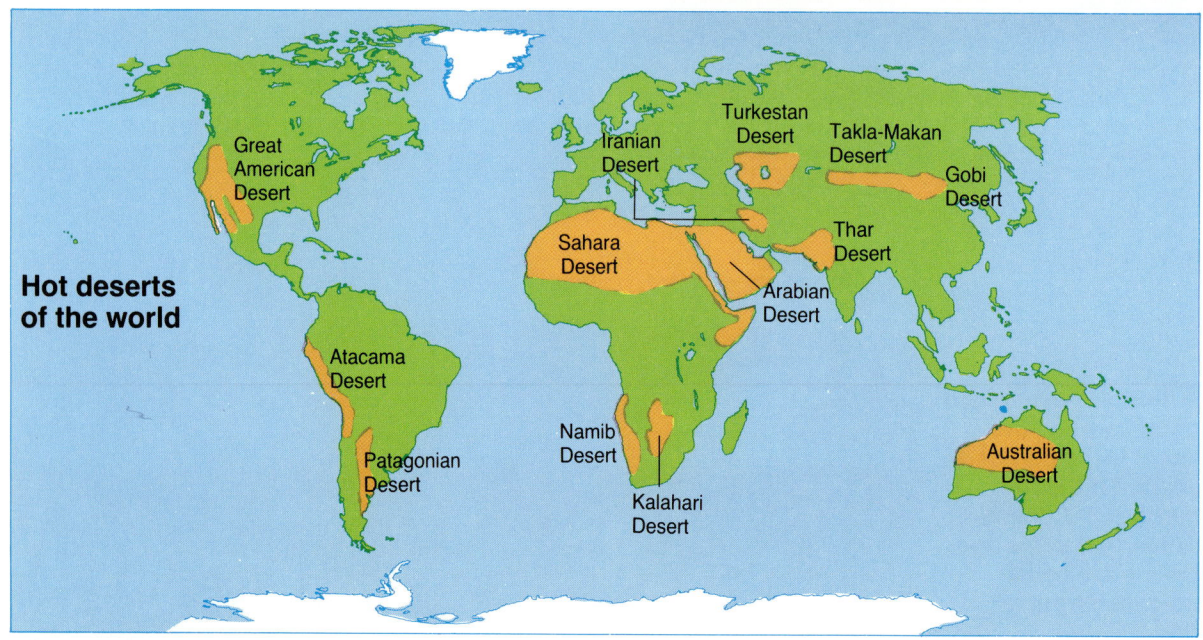

Hot deserts of the world

- Great American Desert
- Atacama Desert
- Patagonian Desert
- Sahara Desert
- Namib Desert
- Kalahari Desert
- Iranian Desert
- Turkestan Desert
- Takla-Makan Desert
- Gobi Desert
- Arabian Desert
- Thar Desert
- Australian Desert

Where do nomads live?

Hot deserts

The hot deserts of the world have less than 25 cm of rain in a year. The **temperature** can reach 57°C in the hot sun. As a result very few plants can grow in these places. Some people and animals have **adapted** to the hot desert climates. To find enough food and water, they have to move across the desert from one well or water hole to the next. There is never enough grass for them to stay in one place. The hot deserts of the world are shown on the map. Each hot desert is different.

Cold deserts

Other parts of the world are very cold and dry. These are the polar deserts of the Arctic and the Antarctic. They are frozen and covered with snow for most of the year.

In parts of the Arctic, some of the snow melts in the short summer. Then mosses and short grass can grow and provide food for some animals. The people who settled in the Arctic lived by hunting the wildlife on the shore and on the ice. They found ways of surviving in the bitter cold.

▲ Nomads called Kurds live in the hot dry deserts of Kurdistan, Iraq. They are cattle herders and live in tents made of goat's hair. For hundreds of years the Kurds have made beautiful carpets and rugs.

▶ Some of the Saami still herd reindeer. They train them to pull heavy sledges over the frozen land. The Saami herders use the reindeer skins to make warm clothes.

Homes and belongings

▼ When the Inuit go hunting in Greenland, they sometimes build snow houses called igloos. They are made from blocks of snow.

Nomads had to travel with very few belongings as they were always on the move. They could not carry many things. They made use of objects that they found to make the few things they needed. They used animal skins to make their clothes and tents. They made spears and tools out of the bones of animals.

Homes in the snow

The Inuit people of the Arctic survived for thousands of years by hunting wild animals. They made skin boats for hunting on the water. They made sledges for moving on the snow. They had different ways of making their houses. In the summer they lived in tents made from seal or reindeer skin. During the cold months they lived in low rock houses. Large slabs of rock covered the roof. Slabs of grass, or **turfs**, were packed all around the house to keep in the heat. They made **igloos** out of blocks of snow when they hunted over the ice in winter.

Today, most of the Inuit have given up their old way of life. They live in wooden houses in towns or in small villages on **settlements**.

Homes and belongings

Homes in the hot deserts

Some of the San people of the Kalahari Desert still make their shelters in the old way. They make a frame of tree branches. Then they cover it with grass. They have made houses this way for 20 000 years. The shelter will only be used for a short time. Then they will move on again in search of food and water.

For hundreds of years the Bedouins of the Sahara and Arabian Deserts made their tents from goat or camel hair. They used to spin and then weave the thread into cloth. They also used to make carpets and rugs for their tents. When they moved on, all their goods were loaded on to their camels.

Travellers of today

Today, people who travel in very hot or very cold parts of the world have copied some of the ways nomads built their homes. They use tents shaped like the homes of the nomads. Scientists in the Arctic use frame tents which are round in shape like the igloos of the Inuit. The round shape is good for keeping in the heat.

▲ This Bedouin woman is spinning thread from animal hair. Some of the Bedouins still make their own tents but many have now settled in houses in the towns and villages.

► These people are setting up camp in northern Canada. They dig holes in the snow. They cover the holes with round, frame tents. Then they pack snow around the outside to keep out the cold winds.

11

Nomads of the cold desert

Thousands of years ago, some groups of hunters crossed into North America from Asia and settled on the Arctic coast. These early nomads depended on animals for food, clothing and shelter.

The Inuit

Some of these nomads learned how to make boats called **kayaks**. These were made from seal skins. They used them for hunting and fishing. They also built sledges and used teams of dogs to pull them. They hunted polar bears and seals on the frozen seas in winter. In summer, they hunted reindeer. These nomads became the Inuit people of Alaska, Canada and Greenland.

Many of the Inuit hunting lands are now being used for mining and oil work. Although the Inuit were paid large sums of money for their lands, many of them cannot find work. For most of them, the old way of life has gone forever.

The hunters

In Canada and Alaska, some Inuit people now live in towns. Others live in villages. All the children go to school. They are given time off every year to go on hunting and fishing trips with their parents. They learn how to hunt reindeer and seals. In this way the Inuit hope to pass on their old skills to their children.

A few Inuit people still hunt all year round. They sell some of the meat and skins. Others hunt at weekends to bring home food for the family. Only a few Inuit have to hunt in order to survive. Some Inuit people have enough money to hire planes for hunting trips. They want to make sure that they can continue to hunt when and where they like.

New ways of hunting have brought new problems. The Inuit can now use rifles, motor boats and **snow machines**. Hunting has become too easy and too many animals are being killed. In Canada, there are laws to stop people killing too many polar bears and walruses. In Greenland, the Inuit have made their own rules. Hunters have to use sledges and dog teams to hunt reindeer. They cannot use snow machines. In this way they hope to stop the number of animals from falling too low. This also helps the Inuit to keep their old skills.

▲ In Greenland, the Inuit live in villages on the coast. The young people are taught how to hunt. They also learn how to throw harpoons and to fish from kayaks.

Nomads of the cold desert

▶ Some of the Inuit people of Alaska use snow machines to reach their fishing grounds. This Inuit is using a power drill to drill through frozen snow to the water beneath.

13

Following reindeer

Reindeer have to move from place to place to find enough food. At first, the Arctic nomads just hunted them. Later small groups of nomads began to move with the herds. They followed the reindeer on the long journeys, or **migrations**, that they make every year. They helped them to cross rivers. They took care of the young calves.

The reindeer gave the nomads all they needed. They had reindeer milk and meat for food. They used the fur for their clothes and the skin for their tents. They made tools out of the bones and the **antlers**. They were able to train the reindeer to pull sledges across the snow.

▲ The herders use a long rope called a lasso to catch the reindeer. They have to do this when they want to pick a reindeer out of the herd to pull a sledge.

◄ In the spring, the Saami take their reindeer herds to new grazing lands. They use snow machines to round up the herds and to keep the animals on the move.

Following reindeer

▶ The Yakuts people of northern USSR breed reindeer on state farms. They may travel by sledge or reindeer. They use a helicopter to travel the great distance to the nearest town.

The Saami

People called the Saami live in the north of Norway, Sweden and Finland. At one time, the Saami were all reindeer herders. Then settlers moved north and built towns and villages. The Saami began to give up their old way of life. Now only one-tenth of the Saami still herd reindeer.

Reindeer are now kept mostly for their meat. The herders move along behind the herds on snow machines. The herding is done by the men while their families stay in the villages. Sometimes the women and children join their men in the summer.

Nomads of the USSR

There are 6400 km of Arctic coastline in the USSR. The groups of nomads who live there are called the Komi, Nenet, Yakuts and Chukchi (*Chook-chee*). Many of them still herd reindeer today. Other nomads hunt and fish.

All the Komi herders have homes in the centre of their land. In the summer, they travel with their reindeer to the Arctic coast.

If the wives go with the herders, the children go to boarding school. During the school holidays they are flown north to join their parents.

Reindeer are also **bred** and herded on state farms. A state farm may have 24 teams of herders. Each team looks after a herd of 2000 or more reindeer. One team might have 13 herders. Each team lives in a large skin and pole tent. Helicopters fly in fresh food and people coming back from the town.

The children of the herders go to school on the state farm. They are taught in their own language and Russian. Later some of them go to reindeer breeding schools. Others may train to become teachers, doctors or scientists.

Life in the Arctic

The Arctic is a huge area of land and sea. It lies around the North Pole. Most of it is north of the **tree line**. There the ground is too frozen for trees to grow. For thousands of years only nomads lived in the Arctic. Today, there are only about 800 000 of these people left. There are, however, about nine million new settlers in the Arctic. Many of them are in the USSR.

The Arctic was once a difficult place to get to. Now planes fly in and out when the weather is good enough. They fly in scientists and oil workers to the oil fields of Alaska. They bring fresh supplies of food. The workers can have the sort of foods they have at home. The planes are also used to bring in medical supplies.

Clothes for the Arctic

The main danger to the workers in the Arctic is when a vehicle breaks down. Then they are stranded far from their camps in the bitter cold. If people are not properly dressed, they can quickly freeze to death.

Special clothes have to be worn at all times. People new to the Arctic must remember to unzip their jackets, or **parkas**, when they start to get too hot. Sweating can be a real danger. When clothes get wet inside, they no longer keep in the warmth.

The Arctic nomads knew how to make the best clothes for life in the cold. Layers of soft fur and seal skin kept them very warm. When they were running or hunting, the loose layers flapped. This stopped the body getting too hot. The Inuit today buy clothes from the towns. Some of them wear jeans, parkas and rubber boots.

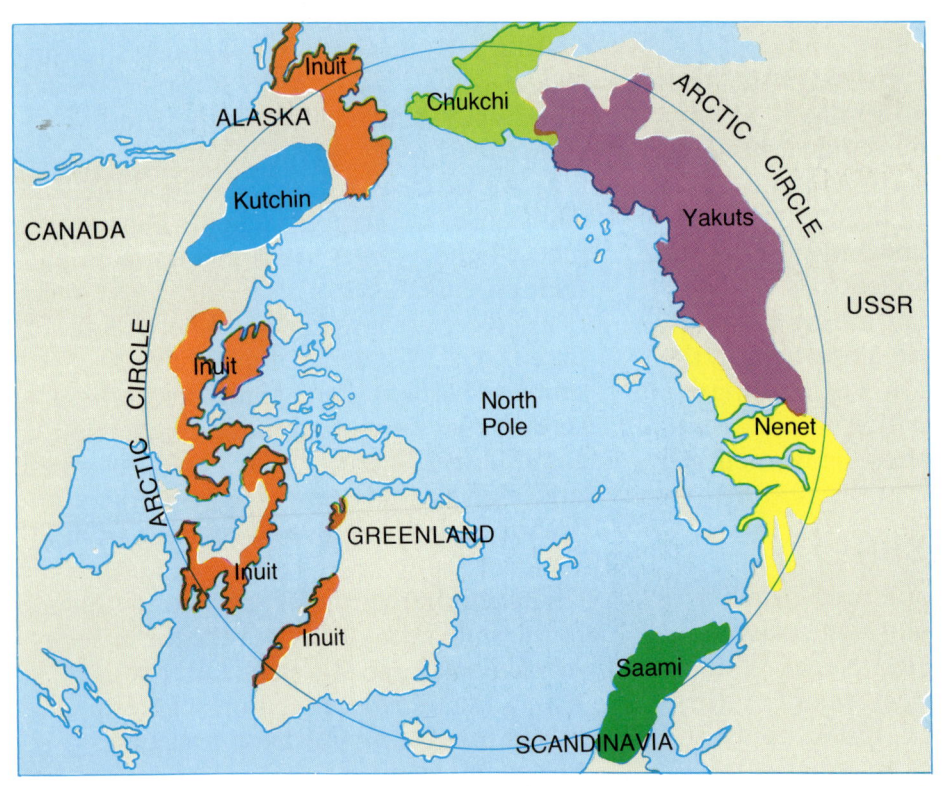

◀ This map shows the land that lies around the Arctic Ocean and the North Pole. There are still a few people who live in these frozen waste lands. Their lands and names are shown on the map. Some of these people live by hunting, fishing and herding reindeer.

Life in the Arctic

▶ This herder is lining his reindeer skin boots with grass. It is a good way of keeping his feet warm and dry in the biting cold.

Migrant workers

Most people who go to work in the Arctic are migrant workers. After a while they will return to their own countries. In northern Canada and Alaska, some teachers live on the Inuit settlements. They usually stay for only a few years.

Scientists may fly in with their tents and **equipment**. Sometimes they just stay for the summer months. Helicopters bring them all the things they need. Oil workers fly to the Arctic from their homes in the south. They may go home for one or two weeks each month. In the Arctic, they live in heated buildings. They have cinemas and television. They have food flown in from the south. All these people are paid very well.

▶ In some parts of Greenland, planes can land and take off on the ice. They bring in supplies and people. The team of husky dogs in the foreground will be used to pull the sledge back to the camp.

Nomads of the hot desert

There is not enough water in the hot deserts for plants to grow. Only a few people live in these hot, dry places. They have to keep on the move to find enough food and water for themselves and their animals.

For thousands of years the desert nomads had the land to themselves. Then oil and minerals were discovered in the deserts. Roads were built to the mines and the oil fields. Oil has brought wealth to countries which were poor before oil was found. Many of the desert nomads have given up their old way of life.

▲ These Aborigine children live on a settlement in the Australian Desert. Some of their food comes from a town 260 kilometres away. They also hunt and gather food from the bush.

◀ Many of the Arab states are now rich from selling oil to the world. They have built new towns and roads in the desert. Here shrubs along the road are being watered from a truck. In time the shrubs will grow and stop sand drifting across the road.

Nomads of the hot desert

▶ In the high deserts of Peru, people keep herds of llamas. Their wool is woven into small sacks which are used to carry goods.

Hunters and gatherers

Today, only a few people live by hunting animals and gathering fruit. Some of the San people of the Kalahari Desert in Africa still live this way. So do a few Bindibu people in the Australian Desert.

The San have no homes and few belongings. Since early times these people have roamed around desert lands looking for food and water. They are able to survive because they know the land so well. The San once wandered over a large part of southern Africa. Much of their good hunting lands have been taken over by farmers.

Herders of the desert

Most of the people who still live in the desert are nomadic herders. They keep herds of camels, goats and sheep. In the Atacama Desert of Chile and Peru, the people keep herds of llamas. All these animals give the herders meat and milk. They can use the skins and wool to make tents and clothes.

The herders often have to travel a long way to find water and grass for their animals. In the spring, goats can get enough water from the plants and roots they eat. In the summer the goats have to be taken to drink at the wells.

The camel has always been an important animal for desert people. Camels used to be the only way of carrying people and goods across the deserts of Africa and Asia. Camels can walk across soft sand without sinking into it. They have large flat feet which spread their weight over the sand. The camel can survive for days without food or water by living off the fat stored in its hump.

Roads have now been built across many deserts. One truck can carry as much as 250 camels used to carry. Some very large trucks are now used in Africa. One of these trucks can carry as much as 4000 camels.

The Bedouin today

▼ Many of the Bedouin still wear their long white robes. Under their head cloth they wear a small cap. Their head cloth is held in place by a black cord. Their clothes keep them cool and protect them from the heat.

The Bedouin people have lived in the deserts of Arabia and North Africa for thousands of years. They travelled around with their herds of animals. All Bedouin people were members of a tribe. Each tribe was made up of several families, with a **sheikh** as leader. He said when it was time to move camp and find new pastures. If the sheikh was rich and strong he might lead several tribes. At one time a Bedouin was rich if he owned a lot of camels.

Oil has made many poor desert countries very rich. They can now afford to **irrigate** large parts of the desert with water so that the land can be farmed. Many of the old Bedouin **grazing lands** have now become good farm land.

▼ Some Bedouin women still wear *burqas* to hide their faces in public. These masks cover all the face except for the eyes. Today many of the women have stopped wearing *burqas*.

The Bedouin today

The town of Rahat

Each year some Bedouin tribes used to cross the Negev Desert in southern Israel with their herds. They thought that they might come back one year and find their grazing land turned into farm land. Some of them camped in tents and got jobs in nearby towns. The Israeli **government** built houses for them. At first, the Bedouin did not want to buy the houses. They did not want to give up their way of life. Bedouins like living close to their relatives.

Then a new town was built to suit the Bedouin way of life. This was the town of Rahat. Each part of the town was kept for one tribe only. Each street was for members of one family. There was enough land with each house to keep a few animals. This new town made it easier for the Bedouin to change their way of life.

▼ **These Bedouins keep falcons for sport. They travel out to the desert from the towns and hunt small birds and animals.**

Customs and changes

Many Arab states have spent a lot of money on houses and schools. All the Bedouin children can now go to school. They learn about different jobs and ways of life.

Life for the Bedouin women has changed also. Many of the young women now wear western clothes. Some of them still wear the dark cloak, or *abaya*, over their clothes. Many of the Bedouin women have stopped wearing the dark mask, or *burqa*. It was worn by some women to cover their faces in public. The long flowing white robe, or *dishdasha*, is still worn by many Bedouin men in the cities.

Falcons have been used by Bedouin people since early times to hunt for food. Wild falcons are caught. Then they are trained to catch hares and desert birds. Many rich Bedouin still enjoy hunting with falcons as a sport. A good falcon may cost a lot of money. Today, it is worth much more than a good camel.

The Tuareg

The Tassili Mountains are in the middle of the Sahara Desert. The mountains are made of a soft stone called **sandstone**. The wind has carved them into strange shapes. Rock paintings have been found in the caves there. They were painted thousands of years ago. They show that people and cows once lived there. The land was not always desert. Today, there is only enough grass for cows far away from the mountains on the southern edge of the Sahara.

The people of the veil

The Tassili and Ahaggar (*Ar-hag-ar*) Mountains have been the home of the Tuareg (*Twa-reg*) people for hundreds of years. These nomadic people were once known as the pirates of the desert. They lived by raiding the camel **caravans** which carried goods across their land.

▲ Many Tuaregs are still nomads. Some of them lead caravans of camels across the desert. The camels carry goods between the desert cities.

▼ Tuaregs herd cattle as well as camels. This water hole is near Agodez in the southern Sahara. Water and fresh grass are hard to find here.

The Tuareg

▲ This Tuareg knows how to survive in the desert, but his jacket and uncovered face show he now lives in the town.

Tuareg means 'people of the veil' in Arabic. The men wear black or blue veils or scarves. These veils are six to nine metres long. They wind them around their heads, and cover the lower part of their faces. A Tuareg man must never show his face to a stranger. The veils protect their faces from the sand and the sun. They wear long blue robes.

The Tuareg women have more freedom than other women in North Africa. They choose their own husbands. They do not wear veils. They read and write the Berber language. The women teach their own children.

The Tuareg today

Today, many Tuareg have settled on farms near a good supply of water. Some of them still live the life of nomads. They graze their cattle and goats on the **semi-desert** lands of the Sahel at the southern edge of the Sahara Desert.

The camel is still important for the Tuareg people. They use them to ride on. The camels carry their belongings and tents. They provide milk, and wool to make cloth. Dried camel skin is used to make water bottles, saddles and sandals.

Some Tuareg people sell cattle in the towns and markets. There they buy rice, sugar and tea, or pots and pans. They do not have many belongings. All the things they own must be carried from one water hole to the next.

Many Tuareg people have suffered from the lack of rain in the Sahel in recent years. Many people lost their animals. There was not enough grass or water for them. Some of them sold the last of their herds to buy houses in villages. Others were left with no animals and no money. Now they camp in tents on the edges of towns.

Living in the Kalahari

▼ These San are digging for the grubs of a desert beetle. They use these grubs to make poison for their arrow heads.

The Kalahari is a huge desert in southern Africa. Small plants, thorn bushes and trees grow in some parts of the desert. These provide food for some animals and for the San people who live there. It only rains there during three months of the year.

By the end of the hot summer the ground is very dry. There is very little food or water left. The San have learned how to survive there. At one time the San lived all over southern Africa. They shared the land with the Khoi people who kept herds of sheep and cattle. Their lands were slowly taken by the farmers who came to the country. Then the San moved deeper into the desert. The farmers did not want the desert land.

The San

Today there are about 50 000 San living in the Kalahari and Namib Deserts. Only about 3000 of these people still live by hunting and gathering. They move about the desert in groups of 12 to 50 people looking for food. During the dry season, when there is less food and water, they split into smaller groups. They move camp when they need to find fresh food and water.

Living in the Kalahari

Most of the San now work on farms and cattle stations for part of the year. Many of them are losing their old skills.

Getting water

In the Kalahari, some rain water collects under the ground. The San are good at finding water in the desert. They dig down one metre. Then they fill the hole with grass to keep the water from draining away. Then they suck the water up through a hollow **reed**. They can also get water from a type of melon and different roots and bulbs. The San use **gourds** and ostrich egg shells to carry and store any water they find.

Hunting

Today, most of the food the San eat comes from wild plants, roots and nuts. The women collect these. They catch small animals like hares, snakes and frogs to eat. Sometimes the men hunt larger animals such as the wildebeest and warthog. They watch and creep up on their prey with great skill. They use bows and poisoned arrows when they hunt.

▲ A group of San women coming back to their camp with food they have picked. The San are now settling on farms. They buy clothes and other goods from local markets.

◄ The San can find water even when it is hidden under the ground. This man is sucking water up through a hollow reed. He will store the water in the ostrich shell.

25

At the edge of the desert

The Sahel is a huge belt of land south of the Sahara. It stretches from west to east across Africa. The Sahel is semi-desert land. It lies between desert in the north and grasslands in the south.

Ten million people live in the Sahel. They have different ways of life. Some people live in small villages. In the wet season they graze their animals there. When it is too dry they travel with their cattle to the rivers. Other people in the Sahel travel all year round with their animals.

There is usually just enough grass and water in the Sahel for all these people. Between 1968 and 1974 there was a very bad **drought**. There was not enough rain. Millions of animals and 250 000 people died. Many of the nomadic herders had to give up their way of life.

▲ The Fulani keep cattle in the semi-desert land called the Sahel. This Fulani herder is playing an instrument made from the horn and skin of one of the animals.

▼ Water is scarce in the desert. There are not many wells or water holes. This one in Chad is 50 m deep.

At the edge of the desert

▲ The people of Mali have used wells like this one for hundreds of years. All the water they need for themselves or their animals has to come from the well.

How herders live

The nomadic herders of the Sahel have to move from place to place all the time. During the dry season they move south to be nearer to the grasslands. They have to use water holes and shallow wells. When the first rains come they move further north to the edge of the hot desert.

The Fulani people roam all over West Africa with their herds. They get most of their food from their cows, sheep and goats. They drink the milk and use it to make cheese and butter. They use the animal skins to make tents and clothes. They also make blankets and rugs.

Nomads at risk

There is always a risk of drought in the Sahel. In recent years the droughts have been getting worse. The nomads cannot find enough water and fresh grass for their animals. If they stay in one place for too long the water holes dry up. The animals eat all the grass. The earth gets broken up by the animals' **hoofs** and the grass roots die. Goats strip the trees and these also die. When it rains there is nothing left to grow. More of the land becomes desert.

It is getting more and more difficult for nomads to live in the Sahel. When the drought is very bad, other countries send them food. Some people go there to help the herders. The herders need to make the best use of the land to stop it from becoming a desert.

Moving with the seasons

▼ In the spring, the plains become too hot and dry for the Bakhtiari and their herds. Then the families migrate with all their animals to pastures in the hills. The journey is long and hard.

Iran is a hot dry country. Some of the people who live there are nomadic herders. These nomads of southern Iran travel long distances with their herds. They have done this each year for hundreds of years.

The Bakhtiari

Each year in the spring, the Bakhtiari and their herds of sheep and goats leave the plains near The Gulf. They begin the long journey to the summer pastures in the Zagros Mountains. There it is cooler and more rain falls.

The people and their animals have to cross six mountain ranges to reach these pastures. They ride horses, donkeys and mules. These animals carry their tents and their few goods. They carry pots and pans, rugs and sacks of grain.

On the journey, they go along twisting tracks and steep paths. They cross the Zadeku pass, which is 4400 m high. There is only enough grazing on the pass for one day. The herds and the people have to keep moving. They travel through snow and the spring flood water. The narrow

Moving with the seasons

mountain tracks are filled with a moving stream of animals and people. Old people, young children and animals all have to cross the mountain streams and rivers. Finally, they reach the summer pastures.

They stay in the mountains for the summer months. In the autumn, when it starts to get too cold for them, the Bakhtiari begin their long journey back to the plains near the coast.

The Basseri

The Basseri people also live in southern Iran. They travel from the low hills north of The Gulf to the mountains further north. They cannot stay in the low hills because there is only enough grass for the herds for three months of the year. During the long summer, the grass dies.

Each year, early in the spring, they start their journey. They go very slowly. The journey can take three months. Sometimes they stop for three or more days at pastures on the way. They do this to give the animals a rest. After a few months in the mountains, it is time to move south again. In this way, the Basseri can find enough food for their animals all year round.

▼ At the end of the summer, the mountains become too cold for the Bakhtiari and their herds. They move back down to the plains again. Donkeys and mules carry the tents on their backs.

A village on the move

Botswana is a hot dry country in southern Africa. Many of the farmers who live there keep cattle. The farmers and their families spend the year in three different places. They live in villages, but they take their cattle far away from the villages to graze at **cattle posts**. They also grow crops on fields a long way from the villages. Farming affects their whole way of life — even the time the children spend in school.

The fields

The rains usually come in October. Then the grass grows. The cattle get plenty of food. They are soon strong enough to be used for ploughing the land. The families leave their villages in November. They go to live in small huts on their fields. They take with them all the things they will need. They stay in the fields until after the **harvest** in June.

Only the children and a few men and women are left in the villages. The children go to school. At the weekends they are taken by truck to work with their parents in the fields. The school term ends in early December. Then the whole family can help with the work in the fields.

School starts again in January. The sowing is over. Some of the women stay in the fields to keep the crops free of weeds. They also have to stop birds eating the young plants as they grow.

The cattle post

The men and young herders take the cattle back to the cattle posts. After the rains there is plenty of grass for them to eat. By April or May the ground starts to get dry. The pools and streams dry up.

▼ After the rains, the herds are taken to the cattle posts. These young herders are herding the cattle across a river in northern Botswana.

A village on the move

The herders have to take the cattle to the wells to drink. The herders have to work hard to stop the cattle from wandering.

In June, all except the young herders move back to the fields for the harvest. The stalks of grain are cut by hand. Then the grain is put into sacks. These sacks are taken back to the village to be stored.

The village

The families come back to the villages after the harvest. If there has been a good harvest there is plenty to eat. The families stay in the village until the rains come again in October. People use this time to do many things. They mend their houses. They make clothes and blankets out of animal skins. They mend their tools and ploughs. When the rains come the families get ready to move. The farming year starts all over again.

▼ In November there are few people in the Botswana villages, only the old people and young children. All the others go to the fields to plant crops.

▲ After the harvest there is plenty of food. The women come back to the villages. They make clothes and bead necklaces to sell in the nearby towns. They also repair their houses with mud or plaster if they have cracked during the dry weather.

Living in the forests

Forest people do not have to travel far to find their food and water. In the forest, there are a lot of animals and fruit for them to feed on. At one time, the American Indians led a nomadic way of life in the cold forests of North America. Now they have settled in villages and towns. They still keep many of their old customs.

In South America, however, there are still about half a million Amazonian Indians who live in the forests. They move from their homes and villages to new homes and villages every few years.

The Amazonian Indians

Rain forest covers a huge area of land around the Amazon River. Groups of Indians live in small settlements by the river or in the clearings in the forest. They hunt animals and gather fruits from the forest. They also grow their own crops.

▲ Amazonian Indians used to paint themselves to frighten their enemies. The colours of the head-dresses are danger colours. In the animal world they mean 'keep away'.

◄ Two or three families may live in a *maloca* like this. They always paint the front of the *malocas* to ward off evil spirits. Each *maloca* has a garden nearby where the Indians grow some of their food.

Living in the forests

▶ This boy is paddling a dugout canoe on the Amazon River. The Indians make these canoes out of a single tree trunk. They hollow out the trunk and then shape it to make a canoe. They use the canoes for fishing.

The Amazonian Indians live together in houses called *malocas*. Two or three families may share one house. The houses are built on wooden frames. The roofs are covered with woven palm leaves. After about five years the palm leaves begin to rot and let in the rain. Then they move to a different part of the forest and build a new house.

Food and farming

The Indians catch fish in the river. They build **dugout canoes** from tree trunks. Some of the Indians hunt birds, monkeys and small animals. They use blow pipes and poisoned darts. Groups of Indians farm the land for most of their food.

Although the forest is green and rich, the soil is very poor. They use a way of farming called 'slash and burn'. Each family group clears a small part of the forest to make a garden. The people cut the wood and burn it. The wood ash makes the soil more **fertile**. They plant many kinds of crop. They grow pineapples, peanuts, yams and manioc for making bread.

After about three years they leave this garden and make another one. The forest grows over the old one.

The future

The Amazonian Indians have lived in the forest for thousands of years without harming it. Now huge parts of the forest are being cut down to clear the ground for roads, mines and cattle ranches. Some of the Indians have left the forest to live in towns or work on the farms and ranches.

The number of Amazonian Indians who live in the forest is getting smaller. Brazil has kept a large part of the forest for the Indians. There they can live as they have always lived.

Working away from home

▼ These migrant workers are about to leave their village to work in Johannesburg. It is too far to travel every day so they do not see their families very often.

People have to work for their living. All over the world there are many people who have to leave their homes to find work. Some even have to go to another country to find work.

Migrant workers

Migrant workers often have to travel a long way from their homes in order to find work. After the Second World War, people were needed to work in the new factories of Europe. People came from Morocco and Algeria to work in France for several months each year. Later, 'guest workers' came to work in West Germany. They came from Turkey and Italy. Some of these workers brought their families and stayed. Most of them went back to their own countries.

Today, thousands of workers go to Johannesburg in South Africa to work in the gold mines. These men have to leave their families in their homelands. There is not enough work for them there. They cannot take their families with them. The men live in **hostels**. Many of them can only go home once a year.

Harvest workers

At harvest time each year, large farms need to take on extra workers to pick cotton, fruit or other crops. In the United States, workers start picking in the south in the early summer. They slowly move north over the summer months. They work on the way.

Each year thousands of fruit pickers live for about five months in camps in California and Florida. Many of these workers are from Mexico.

34

Working away from home

Leaving the land

Migrants from the countryside do not all go to big cities to find work. Some go to new farm lands where there is more work. In South America, many people are leaving the villages of the **altiplano**. This is the high land in the Andes Mountains. It is 4000 m above sea level. The soil is poor. It is hard for the farmers to make a living there. Many of them are now going to work on new farm lands. Some of these are on the Pacific Coast.

Shanty towns

Throughout the world, thousands of people are leaving the countryside. They hope to find work and a better life in cities. Few of these cities can give all these people homes to live in. Many of them now live in **shanty towns** on the edges of the cities. They have to build shelters with anything they can find. They use bits of wood, tin and branches of trees. Some of them look for scraps of metal that they can make into things they can sell. Very few of them are able to find work.

▲ These people have come to work in Florida for the summer harvest. They are picking tomatoes which are then taken to a packing station. When all the tomatoes have been picked, they will move on to work on another farm.

▶ People come to the cities to find work. For many of them, there are no jobs and no houses. They have to make their own houses out of planks of wood or anything they can find. The shanty towns grow larger and larger.

Circus people

For hundreds of years, **acrobats** and **jugglers** travelled from town to town. They used to perform at fairs and markets all over Europe. Then 200 years ago, an Englishman called Philip Astley brought a number of acts together. These people were jugglers, acrobats, clowns and horse riders. He was the first to use the circus ring. He found that trick riders could balance more easily when they rode around in a circle.

▼ All circuses have clowns. They pour water over each other and tumble about. They make everyone laugh.

▲ Inside the big top at Madison Square Gardens, New York, USA. The spotlight is on the trapeze artist. Men hold a safety net in case she falls.

The big top

One hundred years ago, there were many travelling circuses in Europe and the United States. They spent three days to two weeks in each town they went to. They had many different acts. They put on their shows in huge tents. The circus tent was called the big top. The big tops could seat about 5000 people. Teams of tent men were needed to put up these huge tents.

In Europe, the **caravans** were drawn by horses at first, and later by steam engines. In the United States the large circuses often travelled by train. In 1923, two Americans, Barnum and Bailey, called their circus 'The Greatest Show on Earth'. One hundred rail cars were needed to move this show from one place to the next.

Circus people

The circus today

Today circuses are much smaller. The circus owners can no longer afford to pay all the people to put up the huge tents. Gerry Cottle's big top seats 1600 people. When they arrive at a new place, all the circus people help to put up the big top.

During the winter months Cottle's circus sometimes visits other countries. The circus may go to Hong Kong, the Middle East or Singapore. The equipment is sent out by ship. The circus people go by plane. After each tour all the people return to England. They still live in their caravans at their home base.

Circus people feel they belong to the circus. The families travel and stay together. The circus is like a moving village. Gerry Cottle's circus was the first one to provide a school on the move. It is used for the circus children.

▲ Gerry Cottle's circus has a mobile school. The circus children carry on with their lessons wherever they go. The families can keep together as the circus moves from place to place.

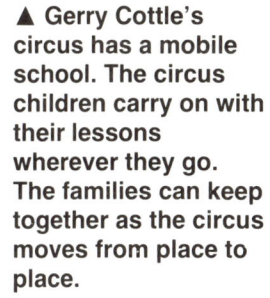

◀ When the circus arrives at a new town, the big top has to be put up. All the circus people help. A power unit is used to lift the huge tent into place.

Music on the move

Musicans have travelled from place to place since early times. Singers and poets used to travel around French courts. **Minstrels** played at fairs all over Europe.

People take their own type of music with them when they go to live in another country. Jazz came from the music brought to the United States by the African slaves. Some of the country and western music came from the folk music of the Scottish and Irish people who went to the United States over 100 years ago.

At one time all music was 'live'. People made music themselves, or they heard it in churches and at fairs. Now there are records and tapes, radio and television. There are musicians who travel around the world because many people still enjoy live music.

Orchestras

A **symphony orchestra** is a large band with 80 to 90 musicians. They play many different instruments. Symphonies are pieces of music written for all these instruments playing together. The players are often away from home. They tour in their own country and all over the world.

The London Symphony Orchestra (LSO) has 84 players. When they go on tour, many things have to be done. Planes and hotels have to be booked. Trucks have to be hired to carry the instruments.

▼ The London Symphony Orchestra has over 80 players and a conductor. The musicians who play the same instruments all sit together. The violins are on the left of the conductor.

Music on the move

The first tour by the LSO in the United States was in 1912. They played 31 concerts in 21 days. Some tours by the LSO can last five weeks. During that time they may visit several countries.

Groups

Today the record industry is big business. Groups who become famous can make a lot of money. Some of them spend a lot of time travelling. From April 1985 to April 1986 a group called 'Dire Straits' did a world tour. They played 270 concerts in 20 different countries. They were seen by two or three million people.

Six of the seven members have homes in the United Kingdom. They do not take their families on tour with them often. The band and their road crew travel by plane, train and coach. They live in hotels. While they are on tour, they have little time to rest. They travel all day and play a concert in the evening. They move on to another town the next day. This goes on day after day, week after week.

When they come back from a tour, they keep on working. They write new songs and make new records. Then they go on tour again.

▼ An evening concert given by the group Dire Straits in front of a huge crowd. They will play for several hours under the hot lights.

Nomads of the stage

Actors and actresses spend a lot of their working life on the move. Some of them travel all over the world. They cannot often find work near their homes.

When a young actress leaves drama school she has to find an agent. The agent is paid to find work for her. She may have to wait a long time before work is found. She has to take the first job she is offered. It may be a small part at a theatre far from her home.

Most well known actors and actresses work in television, films and on the stage. Many of them use the same agent all through their working lives. The agent tries to find work that suits them. Some actors and actresses spend very little time at home. They may only be at home for a short time when they are waiting for the next job to begin.

Nomads of the stage

◀ Part of the film crew on location for the film *Live and Let Die*. They are filming a stunt scene where a power boat leaps out of the water and lands on a police car. About 18 people wait around in the hot sun for the filming to begin.

The stage

At a local theatre, actors and actresses are hired for several months. Sometimes they act in the afternoon and in the evening. In the morning they may be **rehearsing**. They may be learning parts for another play. Sunday is their only day off.

A musical show might start at a local theatre. Then the actors and actresses may go on tour with it. They could take the show to other theatres in different parts of the country. Sometimes a show goes to the West End in London, or to Broadway in New York.

◀ The 'Pirates of Penzance' was first produced by Joseph Papp in New York. In 1982, this musical was performed in London.

On location

A large team of people are needed to make a film. There are actors and actresses, lighting and camera crew. There are **extras** and stunt men, make-up and costume people. Some parts of a film may have to be made on **location** away from the film **studio**. Then a lot of men and women may be away from home for a long time.

Some films, like the James Bond films, have had to be made in many places all over the world. Some of these places may be in very hot climates. A lot of time can be spent waiting for filming to start. It may be pouring with rain or there may be a violent storm. When the weather is right for filming, people may work from sunrise to sunset with little time to rest. This may go on for several weeks.

Nomads of the sea

People who work on ships lead a nomadic life. They all have homes on land but they spend a lot of their working life at sea. Since early times, people have spent long periods of time at sea. The first explorers were away from their homes for months or even years.

It was a hard life on board the early sailing ships. The crew had very little space in which to eat or sleep. Often they did not have enough fresh food. It was a tough, dangerous life. Today, the people who work on ships have a very different life.

▼ The radio operator is always in touch with other ships and with people on shore. All important messages are passed to the captain and the officers on watch.

▲ The chef on a container ship has to cook for nearly 40 people. It is important that he has everything he needs to feed the crew before the ship leaves port.

Nomads of the sea

▲ Dinner is being served to the captain's guests on the cruise liner *Canberra*.

Life on a container ship

Container ships carry their goods in huge containers. They carry their **cargoes** all over the world. The *Resolution Bay* is a British ship. A voyage from London to Australia and back might take three months. The ship calls at different ports on the way. There are 18 officers on board. The officers are made up of both men and women.

There are 19 crew members. Many of them take turns on watch, steering or on deck. They work eight hours a day. They all have their own cabins.

They are away from home for long periods, but there is plenty of paid holiday. The crew get one day of holiday for every three days at sea. During the voyage, when they are off duty, the crew can go ashore to visit the ports. There is a swimming pool and a games room on board.

Life on a cruise ship

The *Canberra* is a cruise ship of the P & O shipping line. Between April and January she cruises all around the Mediterranean Sea. She also visits Norway and the west coast of Africa. A cruise can last from 8 to 22 days. She has a very large crew because she is a passenger ship. The *Canberra* carries 800 crew and 1700 passengers. There is about one crew member for every two passengers. Apart from the captain and the crew who run the ship, there are nurses, doctors, cooks and waiters. There are also people who work in the shops on the ship and musicians who play for the passengers.

The crew have their own games room. They have time to visit ports when they go off duty. For many of the crew, the ship becomes a second home. The officers spend twice as much time on board ship as they do at home. They work for four months at sea. Then they have two months holiday at home.

Nomads of air and space

▼ Muslims come from all over the world to visit their holy city of Mecca. This group from the Netherlands have just landed at an airport in Saudi Arabia.

There are still a few true nomads left in the world today. The Tuareg people of the Sahara still spend their lives moving across the desert. Above their heads in the sky, there are people who live a different kind of nomadic life. These are the men and women who work as air crew. They spend most of their working life flying from one part of the world to the other.

Today, many Arabs go by plane to their holy city of Mecca. Less than 50 years ago they would have travelled by camel. It would have taken them weeks or even months to make this journey across the desert.

Air crews

Air crews earn their living on the world's airliners. They take millions of passengers and cargo all over the world. Some of the passengers may be flying because of their work. Others may be going on holiday.

For air crew, travel is part of daily life. They may spend one day in New York, the next day in London. A few days later, they might be in Australia. The cabin crew take care of the passengers. They serve the meals. The flight crew are the two pilots and a flight engineer.

There may be 11 cabin crew and 3 flight crew on a flight from New York to

Nomads of air and space

Copenhagen in Denmark. The flight takes seven and a half hours. The first stop is London. All the crew leave the plane there and stay overnight at a hotel in London. A fresh crew will join the plane to take it to Copenhagen. The first crew will join another plane to fly back to New York.

Space

A few hundred **astronauts** have now made flights into space. A few of them have landed on the moon. The longest flight in space lasted 237 days. It was made in 1984 by a team of Russians.

Before long there may be **colonies** of people on the moon. There may be giant space stations. People will live and work there for months or even years. The true nomads on Earth are fast disappearing. During the next few hundred years, more and more people will become the new nomads of space.

▲ Edwin Aldrin and Neil Armstrong were the first men to land on the moon in July 1969. This picture shows Aldrin standing on the moon. You can see Armstrong reflected in Aldrin's face visor.

◀ The crew on airliners are the nomads of the air. They travel all over the world because of their work. The flight crew of this plane is made up of a captain, co-pilot and an engineer.

Glossary

acrobat: a person who entertains people by jumping and balancing acts
adapt: to change in order to suit different surroundings
altiplano: level land high up in the Andes Mountains
ancestor: a relative that died a long time ago
antler: one of the two branched horns which grow from the head of deer and antelopes
astronaut: a man or woman who is trained to fly in a spacecraft
breed: to produce young. People breed animals by choosing adults which are special. They may be strong or fast
caravan: (1) a group of people and their camels travelling across the desert (2) a home on wheels
cargo: goods carried by a ship or plane
cattle post: an area of land where cattle can usually find enough grass and water
climate: the usual weather conditions found in an area. Climate differs from one area to another
colony: a large group of people who go from their homes to another place to live and work together
container ship: a ship which carries its cargo in large metal boxes called containers
crop: the plants grown to produce food. Wheat and maize are crops
desert: an area of dry land which has little or no rainfall. Plants cannot easily grow in deserts
drought: a long time without rain
dugout canoe: a long, light boat made from a hollowed-out tree trunk
emigrant: a person who leaves his or her country to live in another country
emigrate: to leave one country to live and work in another country
equipment: everything that is needed for doing a job
extra: a film actor or actress taken on for a short time for a small part
fertile: describes rich soil where seeds and plants can grow well
gourd: a large hollow fruit, often dried and used to hold water
government: the group of people who control a country through laws and rules
grazing land: land where animals can feed on grass
harvest: the gathering of something that has been grown when it is ripe
herder: a person who looks after a flock or herd of animals
hoof: the hard tip at the end of the leg of some animals. Horses, cows, rhinos and antelopes all have hoofs
hostel: a building in which certain people can live and eat. Some students or people working away from home may live in hostels
igloo: a rounded shelter made of hard snow blocks
irrigate: to water dry land using a system of pipes and ditches. The water is pumped from rivers, lakes, or from under the ground. Crops can grow on irrigated land
juggler: a person who entertains people by throwing and catching several objects
kayak: a small boat made of sealskin
location: a place used for making a film away from the studio
migrant worker: a person who travels about to find work, often in another country
migration: the movement of animals over long distances to find food, to breed or to escape cold weather
mineral: any material dug from the earth by mining. Gold, coal and diamonds are minerals
minstrel: a singer or player who travelled around Europe many years ago
nomad: someone who moves around from place to place without making a home in one particular place
orchestra: a large group of musicians who play different musical instruments together
parka: a hooded jacket or anorak
pasture: grassland which animals feed on
rain forest: a type of forest that grows in the tropics where it is hot and wet
reed: a stalk of a tall, thin grass-like plant found by the water or in water. It is hollow inside
rehearsing: practising music or a play before it is performed in public
sandstone: a rock made of tightly pressed sand
semi-desert: land which is dry most of the time but has just enough rain for some plants to grow
settle: to stay in one place in order to make a home
settlement: a small village or group of houses where people want to stay
shanty town: a part of a city where very poor people live. They live in huts or shacks made from any material they can find

Glossary

sheikh: the head man or leader of a group of Arabic people. The word means 'old man'

snow machine: a sledge with an engine used for travel over snow

studio: a room, or set of rooms, where television programmes and films are made

survive: to stay alive

symphony: a large-scale piece of music, usually in four parts. Symphonies are played by a large group of musicians with different musical instruments

temperate: neither too hot nor too cold

temperature: the measure of heat or cold. How hot or cold something is

tree line: the edge of an area in the Arctic above which trees will not grow because it is too cold

turf: a block of grass which has been cut complete with its earth and roots

Index

abaya 21
Aborigine 6, 7
actor 40, 41
actress 40, 41
Africa 19, 24, 26, 30, 43
Ahaggar Mountains 22
air crew 4, 44
Alaska 12, 16, 17
Algeria 34
altiplano 35
Amazonian Indians 32, 33
Amazon River 32
American Indians 32
Andes Mountains 35
Antarctic 9
Arabian Desert 11, 20
Arctic 9, 10, 11, 12, 14, 15, 16, 17
Asia 6, 12, 19
Astley, Philip 36
astronaut 45
Atacama Desert 19
Australia 5, 6, 7, 43, 44
Australian Desert 19

Bakhtiari 28, 29
Barnum and Bailey 36
Basseri 29
Bedouin 11, 20, 21
Bering Strait 6
Bindibu 19
blowpipe 33
Botswana 30
Brazil 33
burqa 21

California 34
camel 11, 19, 20, 21, 22, 23, 44
Canada 6, 12, 17
Canberra, the 43
caravan 22, 36, 37
carpets 11
cattle 4, 8, 23, 24, 26, 30, 31
Chile 19
Chukchi 15

circus 36, 37
circus worker 4, 36, 37
climate 8, 9, 41
clothes 10, 12, 16, 19, 21, 27, 31
Columbus, Christopher 7
container 43
container ship 43
Cook, Captain 7
Copenhagen 45
Cottle, Gerry 37
crops 8, 30, 32, 33, 34
cruise ship 43

Denmark 45
desert 8, 9, 11, 12, 18, 19, 20, 22, 24, 25, 26, 27, 44
  cold 8, 9, 12
  hot 8, 9, 11, 18, 20, 24, 27
Dire Straits 39
dishdasha 21
donkey 28
drought 26, 27
dugout canoe 33

emigrant 5
Europe 5, 6, 7, 34, 36, 38
explorer 7, 42

falcon 21
Finland 15
fishing 12, 15, 33
Florida 34
France 34
Fulani 27
fur 16

gatherers 6, 19, 24, 32
goats 11, 19, 23, 27, 28
gold 7, 34
grass 8, 9, 10, 11, 19, 22, 23, 25, 26, 27, 29, 30
grasslands 8, 26, 27

grazing land 20, 21, 28
Greenland 12
guest workers 34
Gulf, The 28, 29

harvest 30, 31, 34
harvest workers 34
herders 4, 14, 15, 19, 26, 27, 30, 31
herds 7, 14, 15, 21, 23, 24, 27, 28, 29
Hong Kong 37
hoof 27
horses 28, 36
houses 10, 11, 21, 23, 31, 33
hunters 6, 12, 14, 16, 19, 21, 24, 25, 32, 33

igloo 10, 11
India 7
Indians 7, 32, 33
Inuit 10, 11, 12, 16, 17
Iran 28, 29
irrigation 20
Israel 21
Italy 34

Johannesburg 34

Kalahari Desert 11, 19, 24, 25
kayak 12
Khoi 24
Komi 15

llamas 19
location 41
London 41, 43, 44, 45
London Symphony Orchestra 38, 39

maloca 33
manioc 33
Mecca 44
Mediterranean Sea 43
Mexico 34
Middle East 37
migrant workers 5, 17, 34, 35
migration 14
minerals 4, 18
mining 12, 33
moon, the 45
Morocco 34

mules 28
musician 38, 43

Namib Desert 24
Negev Desert 21
Nenet 15
New South Wales 7
New York 41, 44, 45
nomad 4, 7, 8, 10, 11, 12, 14, 15, 16, 18, 22, 23, 27, 28, 40, 42, 44, 45
nomadic herders 4, 19, 26, 27, 28
North Africa 20, 23
North America 6, 7, 12, 32
North Pole 16
Norway 15, 43

oil 4, 12, 17, 18, 20
oil field 16, 18

palm 33
parka 16
pasture 4, 20, 28, 29
Peru 19
plains 28, 29
plants 9, 18, 19, 24, 25, 30
plough 30, 31
poisoned arrow 25, 33
polar bear 12
pop group 39

Rahat 21
rain 8, 25, 27, 28, 30, 31
reed 25
reindeer 12, 14, 15
  breeding 15
  calves 14
  herders 14, 15
  meat 14, 15
  milk 14
  skin 10, 14
Resolution Bay, the 43
rifles 12
rock paintings 22
rugs 11, 27, 28

Saami 15
Sahara Desert 11, 22, 23, 26, 44
Sahel 23, 26, 27
sailors 7, 42, 43
San 11, 19, 24
school 12, 15, 21, 30, 37

scientists 11, 15, 16, 17
seal 12
seal skin 10, 12, 16
semi-desert 23, 26, 27
settlement 10, 17, 32
shanty town 35
sheep 4, 19, 24, 27, 28
sheikh 20
Singapore 37
slash and burn 33
sledge 10, 12, 14
snow 9, 10, 14, 28
snow house 10
snow machine 12, 15
South Africa 34
South America 6, 7, 32, 35
Spain 7
spear 10
spice 7
state farm 15
Sweden 15

Tassili Mountains 22
temperate climate 8
temperature 9
tents 10, 11, 14, 15, 17, 19, 21, 23, 27, 28, 36
tools 10, 14, 31
trade 7
tree line 16
Tuareg 22, 23, 44
Turkey 34

United States 5, 34, 36, 38, 39
USSR 15, 16

warthog 25
water 4, 6, 9, 11, 18, 19, 20, 23, 24, 25, 26, 27, 28, 32
water hole 9, 23, 27
weather 8, 41
wells 9, 19, 27, 31
West Africa 27
West Germany 34
wildebeest 25

Yakuts 15
yam 33

Zadeku pass 28
Zagros Mountains 28